The Movement Through Acts

Workbook

Oscar T. Moses

Sermon To Book
www.sermontobook.com

The Movement Through Acts Workbook / Oscar T. Moses
ISBN-13: 978-1-945793-15-8
ISBN-10: 1-945793-15-5

CONTENTS

The Birth of a Movement (Chapter 1 Questions)

Question: Who wrote the book of Acts?

_____

_____

_____

_____

_____

_____

_____

_____

_____

_____

_____

_____

Question: Why was the book of Acts written?

_____

_____

_____

_____

_____

_____

_____

_____

_____

_____

_____

Question: Who was Theophilus?

_____

_____

_____

_____

_____

_____

_____

_____

_____

_____

Question: What does Jesus say about discerning the time and seasons?

_____

_____

_____

_____

_____

_____

_____

_____

_____

_____

_____

_____

Question: What does Jesus Christ promise His followers in Acts chapter 1?

_____

_____

_____

_____

_____

_____

_____

_____

_____

Question: What does Jesus expect of his followers according to Acts chapter 1?

_____

_____

_____

_____

_____

_____

_____

_____

_____

_____

_____

Question: What did the angel say to those watching Jesus ascent into heaven?

_____

_____

_____

_____

_____

_____

_____

_____

_____

_____

Question: How was Matthias chosen to be a disciple?

_____

_____

_____

_____

_____

_____

_____

_____

_____

_____

_____

_____

Question: Does the church lack power today? Explain your answer with examples.

_____

_____

_____

_____

_____

_____

_____

_____

_____

_____

_____

Action: Individually and as a church, commit today to revisiting the Scriptures, revealing a new reality, releasing God's power in the world, and remembering the end game!

Chapter 1 Notes

_____

_____

_____

_____

_____

_____

_____

_____

_____

_____

_____

_____

_____

_____

_____

_____

_____

_____

_____

_____

_____

_____

_____

WORKBOOK

The Committed Church
(Chapter 2 Questions)

Question: What does 'Pentecost' mean?

_____

_____

_____

_____

_____

_____

_____

_____

_____

_____

_____

_____

Question: Describe the coming of the Holy Spirit in Acts 2:2-4.

_____

_____

_____

_____

_____

_____

_____

_____

_____

_____

_____

Question: Who was present in Jerusalem for Penecost? Name at least five places they were from.

_____

_____

_____

_____

_____

_____

_____

_____

_____

_____

_____

Question: What does the word 'tongues" mean in Acts chapter 2?

_____

_____

_____

_____

_____

_____

_____

_____

_____

_____

_____

Question: What explanation did some of the audience give for what had transpired?

_____

_____

_____

_____

_____

_____

_____

_____

_____

_____

_____

Question: What reason did Peter give to explain why they were not drunk?

_____

_____

_____

_____

_____

_____

_____

_____

_____

_____

_____

Question: What Old Testament prophet did Peter quote?

_____

_____

_____

_____

_____

_____

_____

_____

_____

_____

_____

Question: What was Peter's sermon about?

_____

_____

_____

_____

_____

_____

_____

_____

_____

_____

_____

Question: How did those who heard Peter's sermon feel afterward?

_____

_____

_____

_____

_____

_____

_____

_____

_____

_____

_____

Question: What did Peter instruct the people to do?

_____

_____

_____

_____

_____

_____

_____

_____

_____

_____

Question: How many people joined the church on that day?

_____

_____

_____

_____

_____

_____

_____

_____

_____

_____

Question: What practices did the early church continue steadfastly?

_____

_____

_____

_____

_____

_____

_____

_____

_____

_____

_____

_____

Question: How did the early church show care for one another?

_____

_____

_____

_____

_____

_____

_____

_____

_____

_____

_____

_____

Question: How were people added to church from then on?

_____

_____

_____

_____

_____

_____

_____

_____

_____

_____

_____

_____

Action: Commit today to share Jesus with others, serve in a ministry, and attend church weekly!

Chapter 2 Notes

WORKBOOK

God's Power Presented
(Chapter 3 Questions)

Question: Why did the beggar target Peter and John?

_____
_____
_____
_____
_____
_____
_____
_____
_____
_____
_____

Question: How did God use Peter and John in Acts chapter 3?

_____

_____

_____

_____

_____

_____

_____

_____

_____

_____

_____

Question: What was the reaction of the people who saw the lame man walking in Acts 3:9-10?

_____

_____

_____

_____

_____

_____

_____

_____

_____

_____

_____

Question: What correlation do Acts 3:13-16 have with this miracle?

_____

_____

_____

_____

_____

_____

_____

_____

_____

_____

_____

Question: What contributed to the lame man's healing?

_____

_____

_____

_____

_____

_____

_____

_____

_____

_____

_____

Question: What two commands did Peter give the people?

_____

_____

_____

_____

_____

_____

_____

_____

_____

_____

_____

Question: How was God seeking to bless the people?

_____

_____

_____

_____

_____

_____

_____

_____

_____

_____

_____

Group Discussion Questions

Question: In Acts chapters 3, what role is the Holy Spirit playing in all that has transpired?

_____

_____

_____

_____

_____

_____

_____

_____

_____

_____

_____

Question: Why do you think the beggar positioned himself by the church?

_____

_____

_____

_____

_____

_____

_____

_____

_____

_____

_____

_____

Question: Do Christians limit the power of the Holy
Spirit to help others come to Christ? Explain.

_____

_____

_____

_____

_____

_____

_____

_____

_____

_____

_____

Question: Does God still use Christians to heal in the
same manner today? Specifically, did the Holy Spirit
empower miraculous healings only in the first century to
get the church started, or does He still do so today?
How?

_____

_____

_____

_____

_____

_____

_____

_____

_____

_____

_____

Question: How has the Holy Spirit been active in your life this week? (Ask each person in the group.)

_____

_____

_____

_____

_____

_____

_____

_____

_____

_____

_____

Action: With excitement, a grateful heart, and the help of the Holy Spirit, go forward and witness actively for Christ!

Chapter 3 Notes

WORKBOOK

The Power Resisted
(Chapter 4 Questions)

Question: What was the major problem of Acts chapter 4? Why did the religious officials arrest Peter and John?

_____

_____

_____

_____

_____

_____

_____

_____

_____

_____

_____

_____

Question: Why were the religious officials so upset with Peter and John?

_____

_____

_____

_____

_____

_____

_____

_____

_____

_____

_____

Question: Describe Peter before he received the Holy Spirit. How did he change after receiving the Spirit?

_____

_____

_____

_____

_____

_____

_____

_____

_____

_____

_____

Question: What amazed the religious officials about Peter's sermon?

_____

_____

_____

_____

_____

_____

_____

_____

_____

_____

_____

Question: How did the religious officials try to intimidate Peter and John?

_____

_____

_____

_____

_____

_____

_____

_____

_____

_____

_____

Question: How did the church respond to Peter's and John's experience?

_____

_____

_____

_____

_____

_____

_____

_____

_____

_____

_____

Question: How were the people of the church in "one accord"?

_____

_____

_____

_____

_____

_____

_____

_____

_____

_____

_____

_____

Question: How did the Holy Spirit function in Acts chapter 4?

_____

_____

_____

_____

_____

_____

_____

_____

_____

_____

_____

Question: How can we motivate our church members to be in "one accord"?

_____

_____

_____

_____

_____

_____

_____

_____

_____

_____

_____

Question: What (one) action will your group carry out to assure we are in accord, starting today?

_____

_____

_____

_____

_____

_____

_____

_____

_____

_____

_____

Action: As a church, be in accord and confront resistance confident in the knowledge that the power of the Spirit can't be stopped!

Chapter 4 Notes

Protecting the Integrity of the Church
(Chapter 5 Questions)

Question: How was the Holy Spirit working in the events of Acts chapter 5?

_____

_____

_____

_____

_____

_____

_____

_____

_____

_____

_____

Question: Why do you suppose the couple lied?

_____

_____

_____

_____

_____

_____

_____

_____

_____

_____

_____

Question: How does this passage apply to our church today?

_____

_____

_____

_____

_____

_____

_____

_____

_____

_____

_____

Question: Why did the Lord allow "great fear" in the church?

_____

_____

_____

_____

_____

_____

_____

_____

_____

_____

_____

Question: How does this passage emphasize our need for truthfulness to God?

_____

_____

_____

_____

_____

_____

_____

_____

_____

_____

_____

Question: What message is the Holy Spirit teaching the church about the integrity of a movement?

_____

_____

_____

_____

_____

_____

_____

_____

_____

_____

_____

Question: Acts 5:15 said that people were healed by Peter's shadow. Why do we not see miracles of this magnitude today?

_____

_____

_____

_____

_____

_____

_____

_____

_____

_____

_____

Question: How does Acts 5:16 suggest that the church reach out to the community?

_____

_____

_____

_____

_____

_____

_____

_____

_____

_____

_____

Question: After the church leaders were placed in jail and delivered by the angel, the Jewish council discovered they were preaching again. In verses 26 to 28, the council was very careful not to incite a riot. Why?

_____

_____

_____

_____

_____

_____

_____

_____

_____

_____

_____

Question: What does this chapter teach about obeying God over man?

_____

_____

_____

_____

_____

_____

_____

_____

_____

_____

_____

Question: How is the Holy Spirit empowering opposition?

_____

_____

_____

_____

_____

_____

_____

_____

_____

_____

_____

Question: Who spoke to the Sanhedrin Council on behalf of the church movement?

_____

_____

_____

_____

_____

_____

_____

_____

_____

_____

_____

Question: What does this chapter teach about suffering for Christ?

_____

_____

_____

_____

_____

_____

_____

_____

_____

_____

_____

Group Discussion Questions

Question: What ways can we as a church family resemble the church of Acts 5?

_____
_____
_____
_____
_____
_____
_____
_____
_____
_____
_____
_____

Question: How is the local church harmed from within?

_____
_____
_____
_____
_____
_____
_____
_____
_____

_____

_____

Question: How do we guard ourselves against intimidation in sharing the gospel of Christ, whether in church or outside of church?

_____

_____

_____

_____

_____

_____

_____

_____

_____

_____

_____

Question: How would you describe the "spiritual temperature" of our church? Describe four characteristics.

_____

_____

_____

_____

_____

_____

_____

_____

_____

_____

_____

Action: As an individual believer and as a church, commit to preparing for opposition to the work of the Holy Spirit—but know that the power of the Spirit cannot be stopped!

Chapter 5 Notes

_____

_____

_____

_____

_____

_____

_____

_____

_____

_____

_____

_____

_____

_____

_____

_____

_____

_____

_____

_____

_____

_____

_____

_____

_____

The Source of All Strength
(Chapter 6 Questions)

Question: As the church grew, who complained?

_____

_____

_____

_____

_____

_____

_____

_____

_____

_____

_____

Question: Why was there a need for deacons?

_____

_____

_____

_____

_____

_____

_____

_____

_____

_____

_____

Question: On what did the apostles focus their time?

_____

_____

_____

_____

_____

_____

_____

_____

_____

_____

Question: What are the qualifications of a deacon?

_____

_____

_____

_____

_____

_____

_____

_____

_____

_____

_____

_____

Question: What were the names of the seven deacons?

_____

_____

_____

_____

_____

_____

_____

_____

_____

_____

Question: As word spread and the movement grew, what two things happened?

_____

_____

_____

_____

_____

_____

_____

_____

_____

_____

_____

_____

Question: What did Stephen do among the people?

_____

_____

_____

_____

_____

_____

_____

_____

_____

_____

_____

Question: Who disputed Stephen?

_____

_____

_____

_____

_____

_____

_____

_____

_____

_____

_____

Question: How was Stephen set up?

_____

_____

_____

_____

_____

_____

_____

_____

_____

_____

_____

Question: How did the Holy Spirit present Stephen?

_____

_____

_____

_____

_____

_____

_____

_____

_____

_____

_____

_____

Group Discussion Questions

Question: How does Satan use people to accuse falsely?

_____

_____

_____

_____

_____

_____

_____

_____

_____

_____

Question: What does it mean to be full of faith and power?

_____

_____

_____

_____

_____

_____

_____

_____

_____

_____

_____

_____

Question: How can we, as a church, model this chapter after Stephen?

_____

_____

_____

_____

_____

_____

_____

_____

_____

_____

Question: What three (3) things can you do to model Stephen this Sunday?

_____

_____

_____

_____

_____

_____

_____

_____

_____

_____

_____

_____

Action: God uses ordinary people to accomplish extraordinary tasks. Decide how you will make a stand for the gospel this week!

Chapter 6 Notes

_____

_____

_____

_____

_____

_____

_____

_____

_____

_____

_____

_____

_____

_____

_____

_____

_____

_____

_____

_____

_____

_____

_____

Production Through Persecution (Chapter 7 Questions)

Question: Why did Stephen recount the history of the Old Testament?

Question: What did Stephen imply was wrong with the Jews' attitude about the temple?

_____

_____

_____

_____

_____

_____

_____

_____

_____

_____

_____

Question: Why did Stephen rebuke the council in Acts 7:51?

_____

_____

_____

_____

_____

_____

_____

_____

_____

_____

_____

Question: What is the difference between resisting, grieving, and quenching the Holy Spirit?

_____

_____

_____

_____

_____

_____

_____

_____

_____

_____

_____

Question: Why were these men trying to stop Stephen from speaking?

_____

_____

_____

_____

_____

_____

_____

_____

_____

_____

_____

Question: How did the Holy Spirit empower Stephen in such a cruel death?

_____

_____

_____

_____

_____

_____

_____

_____

_____

_____

_____

Question: What is the importance of Jesus Christ being seated at the right hand of the Father?

_____

_____

_____

_____

_____

_____

_____

_____

_____

_____

_____

Question: What role did Saul play in the stoning of Stephen?

_____

_____

_____

_____

_____

_____

_____

_____

_____

_____

_____

Question: How do Stephen's final words remind us of Jesus?

_____

_____

_____

_____

_____

_____

_____

_____

_____

_____

_____

Question: What the most important lesson can we learn from Stephen, a man who was selected to wait tables?

_____

_____

_____

_____

_____

_____

_____

_____

_____

_____

_____

Action: How can you and your church abandon negative or ungodly behaviors that prohibit church growth? Determine at least one habit your church family should denounce in order to stand more effectively for Jesus.

Chapter 7 Notes

_____

_____

_____

_____

_____

_____

_____

_____

_____

_____

_____

_____

_____

_____

_____

_____

_____

_____

_____

_____

_____

_____

_____

_____

Facilitating the Spread of the Gospel
(Chapter 8 Questions)

Question: Who approved of Stephen's death?

_____

_____

_____

_____

_____

_____

Question: What happened to the church as a result of Stephen's death?

_____

_____

_____

_____

_____

_____

Question: What did Saul do after the death of Stephen?

_____

_____

_____

_____

_____

_____

Question: What did Philip do after Stephen's death?

_____

_____

_____

_____

_____

Question: What results came from Philip's obedience?

_____

_____

_____

_____

_____

_____

_____

_____

_____

_____

Question: Who was Simon the sorcerer?

_____

_____

_____

_____

_____

_____

Question: What happened when Simon encountered Philip?

_____

_____

_____

_____

_____

_____

_____

_____

_____

_____

_____

Question: Why do you think Peter and John had to come to confirm the new believers?

_____

_____

_____

_____

_____

_____

_____

_____

_____

_____

_____

_____

Question: What was Simon's mistake?

_____

_____

_____

_____

_____

_____

_____

_____

_____

_____

Question: How did Peter respond?

_____

_____

_____

_____

_____

_____

_____

_____
_____
_____
_____

Question: How did Philip help the Ethiopian eunuch?

_____
_____
_____
_____
_____
_____
_____
_____
_____
_____
_____

Group Discussion Questions

Question: How does God allow trouble to expand the Good News of Jesus Christ?

_____
_____
_____
_____
_____

_____

_____

_____

_____

_____

_____

_____

Question: How do Christians today suffer for the gospel?

_____

_____

_____

_____

_____

_____

_____

_____

_____

_____

Question: Why is it necessary that someone teach us the Word of God?

_____

_____

_____

_____

_____

_____

_____

_____

_____

_____

_____

_____

_____

Action: Develop a three-step plan to share Jesus in your community!

Chapter 8 Notes

WORKBOOK

Changing Perspectives (Chapter 9 Questions)

Question: What was Saul still doing in Acts 9:1?

_____

_____

_____

_____

_____

_____

Question: What were Saul's intentions?

_____

_____

_____

_____

_____

_____

_____

_____

_____

_____

_____

_____

Question: Why did Saul seek letters from the high priest?

_____

_____

_____

_____

_____

_____

_____

_____

_____

_____

Question: Why do you think believers were called the people of "the way"?

_____

_____

_____

_____

_____

_____

_____

_____

_____
_____
_____
_____

Question: How was Saul persecuting Jesus?

_____
_____
_____
_____
_____
_____
_____
_____
_____
_____
_____

Question: What is the difference between Saul's answer in Acts 9:5 and Ananias's answer in Acts 9:10?

_____
_____
_____
_____
_____
_____
_____
_____

_____

_____

_____

Question: Why was Ananias hesitant to obey Jesus?

_____

_____

_____

_____

_____

_____

Question: According to Acts 9:15–16, what was the call on Saul's life?

_____

_____

_____

_____

_____

_____

Question: What was the Damascus disciple's initial response to Saul?

_____

_____

_____

_____

_____

_____

Question: Why did Saul need to escape?

_____

_____

_____

_____

_____

_____

Question: What reaction did the disciples have toward Saul?

_____

_____

_____

_____

_____

_____

Question: Who spoke up for Saul?

_____

_____

_____

_____

_____

_____

Question: What two miracles were performed at the end of Acts chapter 9?

_____

_____

_____

_____

_____

_____

_____

_____

_____

_____

_____

Question: What was the result of these two miracles?

_____

_____

_____

_____

_____

_____

_____

_____

_____

_____

Action: Share your conversion experience in a small group. Reflect on all of the ways God uses people with a "checkered past" to His greater glory and the growth of the church!

Chapter 9 Notes

Penetrating Prejudices
(Chapter 10 Questions)

Question: Does God want a universal church that encompasses all races? How do you know?

_____

_____

_____

_____

_____

_____

_____

_____

_____

_____

_____

_____

Question: What hinders the reality of a church with all races?

_____

_____

_____

_____

_____

_____

_____

_____

_____

_____

Question: What prejudices do you witness in your church?

_____

_____

_____

_____

_____

_____

_____

_____

_____

_____

_____

Question: What cultural barriers hinder growth in your church?

_____

_____

_____

_____

_____

_____

_____

_____

_____

_____

_____

_____

Question: How can your church become open to the Holy Spirit in a new way?

_____

_____

_____

_____

_____

_____

_____

_____

_____

_____

_____

_____

Action: Brainstorm ways you and your church can be more welcoming to people of different races, ethnicities, and socio-economic backgrounds. Then develop a plan for putting your best ideas into practice!

Chapter 10 Notes

_____

_____

_____

_____

_____

_____

_____

_____

_____

_____

_____

_____

_____

_____

_____

_____

_____

_____

_____

_____

_____

_____

_____

_____

WORKBOOK

Changing Attitudes
Chapter 11 Questions

Question: How did Peter offend the Jewish zealots?

_____

_____

_____

_____

_____

_____

_____

_____

_____

_____

_____

Question: What did Peter rehearse?

_____

_____

_____

_____

_____

_____

Question: How did the Jews respond to Peter's sermon?

_____

_____

_____

_____

_____

_____

_____

_____

_____

_____

Question: What happened to the scattered Christians when they arrived at Antioch?

_____

_____

_____

_____

_____

_____

_____

_____

_____

_____

_____

Question: What happened as a result of the hand of the Lord being with the early Christians?

_____

_____

_____

_____

_____

_____

_____

_____

_____

_____

Question: When the church in Antioch grew, what did the church of Jerusalem do?

_____

_____

_____

_____

_____

_____

_____

_____

_____

_____

_____

Question: What did Barnabas discover when he arrived at Antioch?

_____

_____

_____

_____

_____

_____

Question: Whom did Barnabas seek when he left Antioch?

_____

_____

_____

_____

_____

Question: Where were disciples first called Christians?

_____

_____

_____

_____

_____

_____

Question: What did Agabus prophesy?

_____

_____

_____

_____

_____

_____

_____

_____

_____

_____

_____

Question: What was the response of the church to the prophecy?

_____

_____

_____

_____

_____

_____

_____

_____

_____

_____

_____

Group Discussion Questions

Question: How important is your attitude when God implements change?

_____

_____

_____

_____

_____

_____

_____

_____

_____

_____

_____

Question: How can you help change the negative attitude of people in your church?

_____

_____

_____

_____

_____

_____

_____

_____

_____

_____

_____

Question: How would you describe the hand of the Lord being upon Christians? (What happens?)

_____

_____

_____

_____

_____

_____

_____

_____

_____

_____

Question: What does 'prophecy' mean today?

_____

_____

_____

_____

_____

_____

_____

_____

_____

_____

_____

Action: Align yourself with the Holy Spirit to produce effective change in your life, your church, and your community. Check your attitude about God's preachers, promises, and power!

Chapter 11 Notes

_____

_____

_____

_____

_____

_____

_____

_____

_____

_____

_____

_____

_____

_____

_____

_____

_____

_____

_____

_____

_____

_____

_____

_____

WORKBOOK

The Power of a Praying Church (Chapter 12 Questions)

Question: What was Herod's mission in Acts chapter 12?

_____
_____
_____
_____
_____
_____

Question: Why did Herod seek to kill Peter?

_____
_____
_____
_____
_____
_____

Question: What did Herod do to Peter?

_____

_____

_____

_____

_____

_____

Question: What happened as Peter slept in prison?

_____

_____

_____

_____

_____

_____

_____

_____

_____

_____

Question: What was Peter's state of belief when he awoke?

_____

_____

_____

_____

_____

_____

Question: What did Peter realize after the angels departed?

_____

_____

_____

_____

_____

_____

Question: Where did Peter go immediately after his realization?

_____

_____

_____

_____

_____

Question: What was happening at the place where Peter went?

_____

_____

_____

_____

_____

Question: Who answered the door?

_____

_____

_____

_____

_____

_____

Question: Why did the church not believe it was Peter at the door?

_____

_____

_____

_____

_____

_____

Question: What did Peter do when he went inside the house?

_____

_____

_____

_____

_____

_____

Question: What were Peter's instructions to the church?

_____

_____

_____

_____

_____

_____

_____

_____

_____

_____

_____

_____

Question: What happened when Herod found out?

_____

_____

_____

_____

_____

_____

Question: What did the people say about Herod that made him prideful?

_____

_____

_____

_____

_____

_____

Question: Why did the Lord kill Herod?

_____

_____

_____

_____

_____

_____

Question: What happened after Herod's death?

_____

_____

_____

_____

_____

_____

_____

_____

_____

_____

_____

Group Discussion Questions

Question: Why does God allow "good" people to suffer?

_____

_____

_____

_____

_____

_____

_____

_____

_____

_____

_____

_____

Question: How has the church benefited those in trouble?

_____

_____

_____

_____

_____

_____

_____

_____

_____

_____

Question: Why do you think so many people only turn to the church in prayer when in trouble and never support the prayer ministry when things are going well for them?

_____

_____

_____

_____

_____

_____

_____

_____

_____

_____

_____

_____

Question: Why is it dangerous not to give God glory?

_____

_____

_____

_____

_____

_____

_____

_____

_____

_____

Question: What happens when the church prays in one accord?

_____

_____

_____

_____

_____

_____

_____

_____

_____

_____

_____

Action: Don't fight God or the workings of His Spirit in your life! Instead, trust His leading, and commit yourself to prayer and to helping those who suffer.

Chapter 12 Notes

_____

_____

_____

_____

_____

_____

_____

_____

_____

_____

_____

_____

_____

_____

_____

_____

_____

_____

_____

_____

_____

_____

WORKBOOK

Equipping Those God Calls
(Chapter 13 Questions)

Question: Who separated Saul and Barnabas for an exclusive assignment?

_____

_____

_____

_____

_____

_____

Question: Who was Sergius Paulus, and who was Bar-jesus?

_____

_____

_____

_____

_____

_____

_____

_____

_____

_____

_____

_____

Question: What did Bar-jesus do against Saul and Barnabas?

_____

_____

_____

_____

_____

Question: What happened to Bar-jesus?

_____

_____

_____

_____

_____

Question: Who quit on the missionary journey?

_____

_____

_____

_____

_____

Question: When Paul was invited to speak, what happened?

_____

_____

_____

_____

_____

_____

_____

_____

_____

_____

Question: What is the warning for cynics and skeptics in Acts 13:41?

_____

_____

_____

_____

_____

_____

_____

_____

_____

_____

_____

Question: What did the Jews and religious proselytes persuade Paul and Barnabas to do?

_____

_____

_____

_____

_____

_____

Question: What happened on the next Sabbath?

_____

_____

_____

_____

_____

Question: What was the response of the Jews?

_____

_____

_____

_____

_____

_____

Question: What was the response of Paul and Barnabas after being rejected by the Jews?

_____

_____

_____

_____

_____

_____

Question: Why were the gentiles glad?

_____

_____

_____

_____

_____

_____

Question: How did the Jews get rid of Paul and Barnabas?

_____

_____

_____

_____

_____

_____

Question: What was Paul's and Barnabas's response?

_____

_____

_____

_____

_____

_____

Action: Instead of depending on your own resources, lean on the Holy Spirit and the Word of God to accomplish His purposes in your life and your church!

Chapter 13 Notes

_____

_____

_____

_____

_____

_____

_____

_____

_____

_____

_____

_____

_____

_____

_____

_____

_____

_____

_____

_____

_____

_____

_____

Power, Perseverance, Partnership, and Prudence
(Chapter 14 Questions)

Question: What did the unbelieving Jews do to turn the crowd against Paul and Barnabas?

_____

_____

_____

_____

_____

_____

Question: When Paul and Barnabas learned they were to be stoned, what did they do?

_____

_____

_____

_____

_____

_____

Question: What was the illness of the man in Lystra, and how long did he have it?

_____

_____

_____

_____

_____

_____

Question: What did Paul notice about this man?

_____

_____

_____

_____

_____

Question: What did Paul do for the sick man in Lystra?

_____

_____

_____

_____

_____

_____

Question: After the miracle of the sick man, how did the crowd view Paul and Barnabas?

_____

_____

_____

_____

_____

_____

Question: What was the response of Paul and Banabas after the crowd's reaction?

_____

_____

_____

_____

_____

_____

Question: In Acts 14:15–17, Paul immediately began to elevate God's activity in the lives of all humanity. What was the crowd's response?

_____

_____

_____

_____

_____

_____

Question: After Paul's short sermon, what happened to him?

_____

_____

_____

_____

_____

_____

_____

_____

_____

_____

_____

_____

Question: What happened when Paul reached Derbe?

_____

_____

_____

_____

_____

_____

_____

_____

_____

_____

_____

_____

Question: What did Paul and Barnabas mean by their statement in Acts 14:22?

_____

_____

_____

_____

_____

_____

_____

_____

_____

_____

Question: What was the significance of Paul's and Barnabas's actions in Acts 14:23?

_____

_____

_____

_____

_____

_____

_____

_____

_____

_____

_____

Question: In Acts 14:27, why do you think they gathered the church in Antioch and reported to them?

_____

_____

_____

_____

_____

_____

_____

_____

_____

_____

_____

Action: Look to the Holy Spirit and God's Word for power, perseverance, partnership, and prudence! And reinforce the lessons of Acts so far with this Scripture search:

- Don't quit when times are hard. (Galatians 6:9)
- Trials make your faith stronger: (James 1:2–4)
- Don't force the gospel on people who reject it. (Matthew 10:14)
- Never take credit for what God has done. (Acts 12:23)
- We have a responsibility to know what the Bible says. (2 Timothy 2:15–1 Peter 3:15)
- Be mature in faith. (Ephesians 4:14, Hebrews 5:11)

- Leaders should be tested before being elevated. (1 Timothy 3:1–6, 1 Timothy 5:22)
- Christians should support one another. (Galatians 6:1, John 15:12)

Chapter 14 Notes

_____

_____

_____

_____

_____

_____

_____

_____

_____

_____

_____

_____

_____

_____

_____

_____

_____

_____

_____

_____

_____

_____

_____

_____

_____

_____

Setting Standards for the Saints (Chapter 15 Questions)

Question: What did the visitors from Jerusalem begin insisting of all new converts?

_____

_____

_____

_____

_____

_____

Question: Who resisted these requirements, and why?

_____

_____

_____

_____

_____

_____

Question: Why were Paul and Barnabas sent back to the church at Jerusalem?

_____

_____

_____

_____

_____

_____

Question: What did they do on their way back?

_____

_____

_____

_____

_____

_____

Question: How did the Pharisees disagree with Paul and Barnabas?

_____

_____

_____

_____

_____

_____

Question: When the meeting was called among the leaders, what did Peter talk about?

_____

_____

_____

_____

_____

_____

Question: What was the response of Peter's listeners?

_____

_____

_____

_____

_____

_____

Question: What did Paul and Barnabas say?

_____

_____

_____

_____

_____

_____

_____

_____

_____

_____

_____

Question: What did James say?

_____

_____

_____

_____

_____

_____

_____

_____

_____

_____

_____

Question: What did the group agree?

_____

_____

_____

_____

_____

_____

_____

_____

_____

Question: What did the council's letter say?

_____

_____

_____

_____

_____

_____

_____

_____

_____

_____

_____

Question: What was the response of the new converts?

_____

_____

_____

_____

_____

Question: Why did Paul and Barnabas separate?

_____

_____

_____

_____

_____

Group Discussion Questions

Question: Why is it crucial to understand what God requires of Christians in the Bible?

_____

_____

_____

_____

_____

_____

_____

_____

_____

_____

_____

Question: How should Christians resolve conflict?

_____

_____

_____

_____

_____

_____

_____

_____

_____

_____

_____

Question: How should the church respond to those who give false information?

_____

_____

_____

_____

_____

_____

_____

_____

_____

_____

_____

Question: Who was right between Paul and Barnabas? Why?

_____

_____

_____

_____

_____

_____

_____

_____

_____

_____

Action: Identify some of the standards that the Holy Spirit and the Word set for believers—and commit yourself anew to pursuing those standards with His help! Also seek to resolve conflicts in the church with the help of the Spirit.

Chapter 15 Notes

_____

_____

_____

_____

_____

_____

_____

_____

_____

_____

_____

_____

_____

_____

_____

_____

_____

_____

_____

_____

_____

_____

_____

WORKBOOK

The Holy Navigator
(Chapter 16 Questions)

Question: When Paul reached Derbe, whom did he connect with?

_____

_____

_____

_____

_____

_____

Question: Why was Timothy circumcised?

_____

_____

_____

_____

_____

_____

_____

_____

_____

_____

_____

_____

Question: What did Paul present immediately to those he encountered?

_____

_____

_____

_____

_____

_____

Question: How was Paul directed concerning where he should go?

_____

_____

_____

_____

_____

_____

Question: Who blocked Paul from going to Asia? What other city was blocked to him?

_____

_____

_____

_____

_____

_____

Question: What city did Paul go to after being blocked twice?

_____

_____

_____

_____

_____

_____

Question: Explain the vision Paul saw?

_____

_____

_____

_____

_____

_____

_____

_____

_____

_____

Question: Where did Paul go after the vision?

_____

_____

_____

_____

_____

_____

Question: What happened on the Sabbath?

_____

_____

_____

_____

_____

_____

_____

_____

_____

_____

Question: Who was Lydia?

_____

_____

_____

_____

_____

Question: What happened when Lydia heard Paul preach?

_____

_____

_____

_____

_____

_____

Question: Why did Paul rebuke the slave girl?

_____

_____

_____

_____

_____

_____

Question: Why do you suppose the slave owners had
Paul and Silas jailed?

_____

_____

_____

_____

_____

_____

Question: Describe the events of the night that led up to
the jailor's question, "What must I do to be saved?"

_____

_____

_____

_____

_____

_____

_____

_____

_____

_____

_____

_____

Question: How did Paul and Silas instruct the jailer to salvation?

_____

_____

_____

_____

_____

_____

_____

_____

_____

Question: What was the outcome for the jailer?

_____

_____

_____

_____

_____

_____

_____

_____

_____

_____

_____

Question: What did the jailer do for Paul and Silas?

_____

_____

_____

_____

_____

Question: Why did Paul refuse to be released from prison?

_____

_____

_____

_____

_____

Question: Why were the officials shocked?

_____

_____

_____

_____

_____

Question: Where did Paul and Silas go after being released from prison?

_____

_____

_____

_____

_____

_____

Group Discussion Questions

Question: Are there times when a Christian should compromise his or her beliefs? Explain.

_____

_____

_____

_____

_____

_____

_____

_____

_____

_____

_____

Question: Explain why the Holy Spirit blocks places we would like to go?

_____

_____

_____

_____

_____

_____

_____

_____

_____

_____

_____

Question: Why is it often difficult for Christians to interact with those who are involved in the occult?

_____

_____

_____

_____

_____

_____

_____

_____

_____

_____

_____

Question: How do you respond to people who tell you they can predict your future?

_____

_____

_____

_____

_____

_____

_____

_____

_____

_____

_____

Question: How do we know when the Holy Spirit is leading or whether some other spirit has taken control?

_____

_____

_____

_____

_____

_____

_____

_____

_____

_____

_____

Action: The apostles didn't view circumcision as a duty of the law. Rather, there were unbelieving Jews who would not suffer an uncircumcised person to teach in the synagogues. Timothy was thus limited (1 Corinthians 9:20) because his father was Greek and mothers do not circumcise their sons. With this in mind, identify and commit to at least one inconvenient practice that you can adopt—not because it's necessary, but because it's helpful to bringing others to Christ.

Chapter 16 Notes

_____

_____

_____

_____

_____

_____

_____

_____

_____

_____

_____

_____

_____

_____

_____

_____

_____

_____

_____

_____

_____

_____

_____

The Holy Spirit Reasons (Chapter 17 Questions)

Question: Why did Paul and his companions stop at Thessalonica?

_____

_____

_____

_____

_____

_____

Question: What did Paul reason from the Scriptures?

_____

_____

_____

_____

_____

_____

Question: Why were some of the staunch Jews jealous?

_____

_____

_____

_____

_____

_____

Question: What did the staunch Jews do when Paul and Silas won over new converts?

_____

_____

_____

_____

_____

_____

Question: What were the brawlers doing?

_____

_____

_____

_____

_____

Question: Whose house was broken into?

_____

_____

_____

_____

_____

_____

Question: What did the crowd do to Jason and some other Christians?

_____

_____

_____

_____

_____

_____

Question: What was Jason accused of doing?

_____

_____

_____

_____

_____

_____

Question: When did Paul and Silas leave Thessalonica?

_____

_____

_____

_____

_____

_____

Question: How were the Bereans different from the Thessalonians?

_____

_____

_____

_____

_____

_____

Question: Why did Paul leave Berea?

_____

_____

_____

_____

_____

_____

Question: What did Paul discover in Athens?

_____

_____

_____

_____

_____

_____

Question: Why did the Council of the Areopagus want to hear what Paul had to say?

_____

_____

_____

_____

_____

_____

Question: Why did the Athenians have an altar dedicated to an "unknown god"?

_____

_____

_____

_____

_____

Question: How did Paul prove that God was not and idol?

_____

_____

_____

_____

_____

_____

_____

_____

_____

_____

_____

Question: How did the Greeks respond to Paul?

_____

_____

_____

_____

_____

_____

Question: Who among Paul's hearers become believers?

_____

_____

_____

_____

_____

Group Discussion Questions

Question: If you were involved in a small-group Bible study, which would you prefer to be: a teacher or one of the students? Why?

_____

_____

_____

_____

_____

_____

_____

_____

_____

_____

Question: Name two (2) things you can do to make the gospel message heard to your non-Christian friends and co-workers.

_____

_____

_____

_____

_____

_____

_____

_____

_____

_____

Question: The church at Berea searched the scriptures daily. What can be done at your church to generate inspiration to study God's Word?

_____

_____

_____

_____

_____

_____

_____

_____

_____

_____

_____

Question: Would you say that your church is a Bible teaching church? Explain.

_____

_____

_____

_____

_____

_____

_____

_____

_____

_____

_____

Action: This week, put into practice at least one of your ideas for reaching a non-Christian friend or co-worker.

Chapter 17 Notes

_____

_____

_____

_____

_____

_____

_____

_____

_____

_____

_____

_____

_____

_____

_____

_____

_____

_____

_____

_____

_____

_____

_____

_____

Affirmation, Assurance, and Assistance (Chapter 18 Questions)

Question: What did Paul have in common with Aquila and Priscilla?

_____

_____

_____

_____

_____

_____

Question: Why was Paul in the synagogue every Sabbath?

_____

_____

_____

_____

_____

_____

Question: Who came from Macedonia?

_____

_____

_____

_____

_____

_____

Question: When the Jews opposed Paul's witness of Christ, what did he do?

_____

_____

_____

_____

_____

_____

_____

_____

_____

_____

Question: Why was Paul able to stop tent-making when his friends arrived from Macedonia?

_____

_____

_____

_____

_____

_____

_____

_____

_____

_____

_____

_____

Question: To whose house did Paul go when he left the synagogue?

_____

_____

_____

_____

_____

_____

Question: What happened to the leader or chief ruler of the synagogue and his family?

_____

_____

_____

_____

_____

_____

_____

_____

_____

_____

_____

Question: What did many of the Corinthians do?

_____

_____

_____

_____

_____

Question: What did the Lord tell Paul in a night vision?

_____

_____

_____

_____

_____

_____

_____

_____

_____

_____

Question: How long did Paul stay in Corinth after the night vision?

_____

_____

_____

_____

_____

_____

Question: What happened when Gallio was deputy of Achaia?

_____

_____

_____

_____

_____

_____

_____

_____

_____

_____

_____

Question: What happened as Paul began to defend himself?

_____

_____

_____

_____

_____

_____

Question: What happened to the new temple leader, Sosthenes? Why?

_____

_____

_____

_____

_____

Question: When Paul left Corinth, whom did he take with him?

_____

_____

_____

_____

_____

Question: As soon as Paul got off the ship in Ephesus, what did he do?

_____

_____

_____

_____

_____

Question: Where did Paul go from Ephesus?

_____

_____

_____

_____

_____

_____

Question: After Paul left Antioch, what did he do?

_____

_____

_____

_____

_____

_____

Question: Who was Apollos?

_____

_____

_____

_____

_____

_____

Question: How was Apollos limited in the Scriptures?

_____

_____

_____

_____

_____

_____

Question: Who gently corrected Apollos?

_____

_____

_____

_____

_____

_____

Question: How did Apollos put his gifts and knowledge to good use?

_____

_____

_____

_____

_____

_____

_____

_____

_____

_____

Question: How did Apollos serve God with his skills and abilities?

_____

_____

_____

_____

_____

_____

_____

_____

_____

_____

_____

_____

Question: How did God use Apollos in Achaia?

_____

_____

_____

_____

_____

_____

_____

_____

_____

_____

Question: What approach did Apollos use in defending the Christian faith?

_____

_____

_____

_____

_____

_____

_____

_____

_____

_____

_____

_____

Group Discussion Questions

Question: How does the Holy Spirit affirm us in the face of conflict?

_____

_____

_____

_____

_____

_____

_____

_____

_____

_____

_____

_____

Question: What would happen if the church did not financially support ministry?

_____

_____

_____

_____

_____

_____

_____

_____

_____

_____

_____

Question: What freedoms do we tend to take for granted with regard to practicing our faith, in contrast to believers in other times and places?

_____

_____

_____

_____

_____

_____

_____

_____

_____

_____

_____

Question: When you are discouraged, how does the Holy Spirit give you assurance?

_____

_____

_____

_____

_____

_____

_____

_____

_____

_____

_____

Question: How do you correct someone who has erred in the Scriptures?

_____

_____

_____

_____

_____

_____

_____

_____

_____

_____

_____

Question: How does the Holy Spirit assist in ministry?

_____

_____

_____

_____

_____

_____

_____

_____

_____

_____

_____

_____

Action: Look to the Holy Spirit for help in correcting fellow believers in their spiritual errors—with an attitude of humility and godly love.

Chapter 18 Notes

_____

_____

_____

_____

_____

_____

_____

_____

_____

_____

_____

_____

_____

_____

_____

_____

_____

_____

_____

_____

_____

_____

WORKBOOK

Victorious over the Occult
(Chapter 19 Questions)

Question: What did Paul ask the disciples at Ephesus?

_____

_____

_____

_____

_____

_____

Question: What was their response to Paul's question?

_____

_____

_____

_____

_____

Question: What was the difference between John's baptism and baptism in the name of Jesus?

_____

_____

_____

_____

_____

_____

_____

_____

_____

_____

_____

_____

Question: What happened after they were baptized in the name of Jesus?

_____

_____

_____

_____

_____

Question: How long did Paul teach at the synagogue before trouble arose?

_____

_____

_____

_____

_____

Question: What happened with Paul's garments?

_____

_____

_____

_____

_____

_____

Question: Why did the people far and wide praise Jesus?

_____

_____

_____

_____

_____

_____

Question: How did Paul's teaching of Jesus Christ change the people drastically in Ephesus?

_____

_____

_____

_____

_____

_____

_____

_____

_____

_____

_____

Question: How was Christianity spread? (See Acts 19:20.)

_____

_____

_____

_____

_____

_____

_____

_____

_____

_____

Question: What city did Paul want to see?

_____

_____

_____

_____

_____

Question: Who was referred to as "the Way"?

_____

_____

_____

_____

_____

_____

Question: Who led the opposition against Paul and the Christians? Why?

_____

_____

_____

_____

_____

_____

Question: Why did the silversmith's talk create such a commotion?

_____

_____

_____

_____

_____

_____

Question: Why did the crowd take two of Paul's men?

_____

_____

_____

_____

_____

_____

Question: How did the town clerk calm the crowd down?

_____

_____

_____

_____

_____

_____

Group Discussion Questions

Question: Why should Christians refrain from buying prayer or healing clothes from television?

_____

_____

_____

_____

_____

_____

_____

_____

_____

_____

_____

Question: Should Christians read their horoscope?

_____

_____

_____

_____

_____

_____

_____

_____

_____

_____

_____

Question: How does the gospel change lives when taught?

_____

_____

_____

_____

_____

_____

_____

_____

_____

_____

Question: How has the Word of God changed your life?

_____

_____

_____

_____

_____

_____

_____

_____

_____

_____

_____

_____

_____

Action: Keep a sharp eye and prayerful mind with regard to spiritually dangerous influences in your home, workplace, and entertainment. Commit today to separating yourself from those spiritual traps!

Chapter 19 Notes

_____

_____

_____

_____

_____

_____

_____

_____

_____

_____

_____

_____

_____

_____

_____

_____

_____

_____

_____

_____

_____

_____

_____

Empowering the Saints to Completion (Chapter 20 Questions)

Question: What did Paul do after the uproar in Ephesus was over?

_____

_____

_____

_____

_____

_____

Question: Where did Paul stay for three months?

_____

_____

_____

_____

_____

_____

Question: How was Paul's plan to sail to Syria frustrated?

_____

_____

_____

_____

_____

_____

Question: When did the Christians meet to break bread?

_____

_____

_____

_____

_____

_____

Question: What happened when Eutychus fell asleep?

_____

_____

_____

_____

_____

_____

Question: Why were the people comforted when they took Eutychus home?

_____

_____

_____

_____

_____

_____

Question: Why was Paul in a hurry to get to Jerusalem?

_____

_____

_____

_____

_____

Question: Why did Paul expect trouble in Jerusalem?

_____

_____

_____

_____

_____

Question: What mattered most to Paul? (See Acts 20:24.)

_____

_____

_____

_____

_____

Question: In what did Paul not fail, as he reminded the congregation?

_____

_____

_____

_____

_____

_____

Question: What were the future responsibilities of the Ephesian elders?

_____

_____

_____

_____

_____

_____

_____

_____

_____

_____

_____

Question: How did the elders display their deep love for Paul?

_____

_____

_____

_____

_____

Question: What saddened the group most?

_____

_____

_____

_____

_____

_____

Group Discussion Questions

Question: How do you want to be remembered?

_____

_____

_____

_____

_____

_____

_____

_____

_____

_____

_____

Question: Will you be a good memory?

_____
_____
_____
_____
_____
_____
_____
_____
_____
_____
_____

Question: Whom have you trained to carry on your ministry?

_____
_____
_____
_____
_____
_____
_____
_____
_____
_____
_____

Question: How many times have you quit?

_____

_____

_____

_____

_____

_____

_____

_____

_____

_____

_____

Question: How do you keep from quitting?

_____

_____

_____

_____

_____

_____

_____

_____

_____

_____

_____

_____

Question: Can you continue to be faithful even when you know harm lies ahead?

_____

_____

_____

_____

_____

_____

_____

_____

_____

_____

_____

_____

Question: How has false doctrine entered the church?

_____

_____

_____

_____

_____

_____

_____

_____

_____

_____

_____

Question: Why do you think so many people accept beliefs that the Bible does not confirm?

_____

_____

_____

_____

_____

_____

_____

_____

_____

_____

_____

_____

Action: Keep track of false doctrines or beliefs you encounter this week in your workplace, your community, and the media. Then look to the Spirit and the Word and come up with a plan to counter each of those false beliefs!

Chapter 20 Notes

_____

_____

_____

_____

_____

_____

_____

_____

_____

_____

_____

_____

_____

_____

_____

_____

_____

_____

_____

_____

_____

_____

_____

The Sustainer of Ministry
(Chapter 21 Questions)

Question: What did Paul and his companions find in Patara?

_____

_____

_____

_____

_____

_____

Question: Whom did Paul and his companions discover in Tyre?

_____

_____

_____

_____

_____

_____

Question: What was Paul advised?

_____

_____

_____

_____

_____

_____

Question: What did Paul tell the people of Tyre as he was about to depart?

_____

_____

_____

_____

_____

_____

Question: Whose house did Paul enter when they reached Caesarea?

_____

_____

_____

_____

_____

_____

Question: How many daughters did he have, and how does the Bible describe them?

_____

_____

_____

_____

_____

_____

Question: Who was Agabus, and what did he do?

_____

_____

_____

_____

_____

_____

Question: What did the people advise Paul not to do?

_____

_____

_____

_____

_____

_____

Question: What was Paul's response?

_____

_____

_____

_____

_____

_____

Question: What was the name of the old disciple with whom Paul stayed?

_____

_____

_____

_____

_____

_____

Question: What happened when Paul met with James?

_____

_____

_____

_____

_____

_____

_____

_____

_____

_____

Question: Why were the brethren upset?

_____

_____

_____

_____

_____

_____

Question: What did they advise Paul to do with four men?

_____

_____

_____

_____

_____

_____

Question: After the seven days ended, what did the Jews from Asia do to Paul?

_____

_____

_____

_____

_____

_____

Question: What was their accusation against Paul?

_____

_____

_____

_____

_____

_____

Question: How was Paul's life spared?

_____

_____

_____

_____

_____

_____

Question: While bound in chains, what did Paul say to
the chief captain?

_____

_____

_____

_____

_____

_____

Question: Why was the chief captain surprised?

_____

_____

_____

_____

_____

Question: What did Paul ask permission of the chief
captain to do?

_____

_____

_____

_____

_____

_____

Question: How does Acts chapter 21 conclude?

_____

_____

_____

_____

_____

_____

_____

_____

_____

_____

_____

Group Discussion Questions

Question: Have you ever gone against the advice of others because the Holy Spirit led you? Explain.

_____

_____

_____

_____

_____

_____

_____

_____

_____

_____

_____

Question: Are there instances when compromise is necessary to keep the peace?

_____

_____

_____

_____

_____

_____

_____

_____

_____

_____

Question: When should you adjust your behavior for the sake of others?

_____

_____

_____

_____

_____

_____

_____

_____

_____

_____

_____

Question: What are some examples of false information
about Christianity that has been widely spread?

_____

_____

_____

_____

_____

_____

_____

_____

_____

_____

Question: What made Paul so determined?

_____

_____

_____

_____

_____

_____

_____

_____

_____

_____

_____

Action: This week, begin a daily habit of prayer whenever you find yourself caught in a misunderstanding or conflict. Seek guidance from the Lord, His Spirit, and His Word as to whether and how you need to compromise—or stand firm!

Chapter 21 Notes

_____

_____

_____

_____

_____

_____

_____

_____

_____

_____

_____

_____

_____

_____

_____

_____

_____

_____

_____

_____

_____

_____

_____

The Power of Personal Testimonies (Chapter 22 Questions)

Question: Why did the crowd get silent when they heard Paul speak?

_____

_____

_____

_____

_____

_____

Question: Who did Paul say was his teacher?

_____

_____

_____

_____

_____

_____

Question: What did Paul say he once did?

_____

_____

_____

_____

_____

_____

Question: What happened to Paul on the Damascus road?

_____

_____

_____

_____

_____

_____

_____

_____

_____

_____

_____

Question: Where did the Lord Jesus instruct Paul to go for further instructions?

_____

_____

_____

_____

_____

Question: What devout man came to Paul in Damascus?

_____

_____

_____

_____

_____

_____

Question: What were Ananias's instructions from the Lord?

_____

_____

_____

_____

_____

_____

_____

_____

_____

_____

Question: Why did Jesus instruct Paul to leave Jerusalem?

_____

_____

_____

_____

_____

Question: To whom was Paul assigned to witness?

_____

_____

_____

_____

_____

_____

Question: What was the crowd's response to Paul?

_____

_____

_____

_____

_____

Question: How did Paul avoid the scourging?

_____

_____

_____

_____

_____

Question: Why was the chief captain fearful?

_____

_____

_____

_____

_____

Question: What happened the next day?

_____

_____

_____

_____

_____

_____

_____

_____

_____

_____

_____

Group Discussion Questions

Question: What ways can you adjust your speech to deal with hostile personalities?

_____

_____

_____

_____

_____

_____

_____

_____

_____

_____

_____

Question: What do you think most people want to hear when you are trying to win them to Christ? What do they not want to hear?

_____

_____

_____

_____

_____

_____

_____

_____

_____

_____

_____

Question: Why should every Christian be able to talk about Jesus Christ?

_____

_____

_____

_____

_____

_____

_____

_____

_____

_____

_____

_____

Action: Based on what you have learned about a Christian testimony, write or type at least one page describing your testimony. Be sure to include:

1. Who were you before you came to know Jesus Christ?
2. How did you come to know Jesus Christ?
3. How has your life changed since you met Jesus Christ?

Chapter 22 Notes

_____

_____

_____

_____

_____

_____

_____

_____

_____

_____

_____

_____

_____

_____

_____

_____

_____

_____

_____

_____

_____

_____

WORKBOOK

Courage to Stay the Course (Chapter 23 Questions)

Question: What did Paul tell the council he had done as far as his conscience?

_____

_____

_____

_____

_____

_____

Question: How did the chief priest respond?

_____

_____

_____

_____

_____

_____

_____

_____

_____

_____

_____

Question: How did Paul respond to the chief priest's actions?

_____

_____

_____

_____

_____

_____

_____

_____

_____

_____

Question: Was Paul aware of what he had done?

_____

_____

_____

_____

_____

_____

Question: How did Paul divide the crowd?

_____

_____

_____

_____

_____

_____

Question: What differences did the Pharisees and Saducees have concerning the resurrection?

_____

_____

_____

_____

_____

_____

_____

_____

_____

_____

_____

Question: Why was Paul removed from the crowd?

_____

_____

_____

_____

_____

_____

214 · OSCAR T. MOSES

Question: How did Jesus affirm Paul?

_____

_____

_____

_____

_____

_____

_____

Question: What did some men vow to do? Who told Paul of the plot?

_____

_____

_____

_____

_____

_____

Question: What did this young man do privately?

_____

_____

_____

_____

_____

_____

Question: What did the captain tell Paul's nephew?

_____

_____

_____

_____

_____

_____

Question: How was Paul presented safely to Felix?

_____

_____

_____

_____

_____

_____

_____

_____

_____

_____

_____

Question: To whom did the captain write a letter?

_____

_____

_____

_____

_____

_____

Question: What did the letter say?

_____

_____

_____

_____

_____

_____

_____

_____

_____

_____

_____

_____

Question: How does this chapter end for Paul?

_____

_____

_____

_____

_____

_____

_____

_____

_____

_____

_____

_____

Group Discussion Questions

Question: What should we do when crisis and criticism surface in our lives? How do you examine your conscience?

_____

_____

_____

_____

_____

_____

_____

_____

_____

_____

Question: How will you do the right thing despite the cost?

_____

_____

_____

_____

_____

_____

_____

_____

_____

_____

_____

Question: How will you stand alone when needed?

_____

_____

_____

_____

_____

_____

_____

_____

_____

_____

Question: How will you stay the course through trials?

_____

_____

_____

_____

_____

_____

_____

_____

_____

_____

Action: Make a habit of prayerfully examining your conscience and reflecting on your relationship with God. Remember, as Paul teaches us, that the Holy Spirit will assist us in fighting spiritual battles, keeping the faith, and finishing our course (see 2 Timothy 4:7, John 19:30). Spend time praying for the help of the Holy Spirit in standing your spiritual ground when He calls you to do so!

Chapter 23 Notes

_____

_____

_____

_____

_____

_____

_____

_____

_____

_____

_____

_____

_____

_____

_____

_____

_____

_____

_____

_____

_____

_____

WORKBOOK

A Christian Character and a Clear Conscience (Chapter 24 Questions)

Question: With whom did Ananias appear after five days?

_____

_____

_____

_____

_____

_____

Question: What were this man's charges against Paul?

_____

_____

_____

_____

_____

_____

Question: How did the Jews respond to the charges?

_____

_____

_____

_____

_____

_____

_____

_____

_____

_____

Question: What was Paul's response?

_____

_____

_____

_____

_____

_____

_____

_____

_____

_____

Question: What did Paul say he came to bring to the nations?

_____

_____

_____

_____

_____

_____

Question: Who did Paul say started all of the trouble?

_____

_____

_____

_____

_____

_____

Question: How did Felix respond to Paul's defense?

_____

_____

_____

_____

_____

_____

_____

_____

_____

_____

_____

Question: What happened when Felix and his wife Drusilla sent for Paul? What was Felix's response?

_____

_____

_____

_____

_____

_____

_____

_____

_____

_____

_____

Question: What was Felix hoping Paul would do for him?

_____

_____

_____

_____

_____

Question: Who replaced Felix?

_____

_____

_____

_____

_____

Question: How does this chapter end for Paul?

_____

_____

_____

_____

_____

_____

_____

_____

_____

_____

_____

Group Discussion Questions

Question: Is your conscience clear before God? Explain.

_____

_____

_____

_____

_____

_____

_____

_____

_____

_____

_____

Question: Is your conscience clear on the work you do for the Kingdom of God? Explain.

_____

_____

_____

_____

_____

_____

_____

_____

_____

_____

_____

Question: Do you feed the hungry, clothe the naked, and visit the sick as Christ has commanded? What are some specific steps you could take to begin doing more of the things He requires us to do?

_____

_____

_____

_____

_____

_____

_____

_____

_____

_____

_____

Question: Is your conscience clear on your level of worship before God? Do you give God adequate worship time? Explain.

_____

_____

_____

_____

_____

_____

_____

_____

_____

Question: When, where, and how often do you pray? How could you grow in the discipline of prayer?

_____

_____

_____

_____

_____

_____

_____

_____

_____

_____

Question: Is your conscience clear to stand before God on the tithe? Explain.

_____

_____

_____

_____

_____

_____

_____

_____

_____

_____

_____

Question: Is your conscience clear on witnessing? How could you witness more effectively?

_____

_____

_____

_____

_____

_____

_____

_____

_____

_____

_____

Question: Have you adequately shared the gospel? How could you share the gospel more effectively?

_____

_____

_____

_____

_____

_____

_____

_____

_____

_____

_____

Question: Is your conscience clear on your level of knowledge about God's Word? How could you grow in your knowledge of the Word?

_____

_____

_____

_____

_____

_____

_____

_____

_____

_____

Action: Make a list of characteristics that define a Christian character, and keep it close at hand this week. Pray to God for the help of His Holy Spirit in pursuing a Christian character daily!

Chapter 24 Notes

_____

_____

_____

_____

_____

_____

_____

_____

_____

_____

_____

_____

_____

_____

_____

_____

_____

_____

_____

_____

_____

_____

_____

The Provider of Patience (Chapter 25 Questions)

Question: What happened when Festus came to the province?

_____
_____
_____
_____
_____
_____

Question: Why were the Jewish leaders trying to get Festus to send Paul to Jerusalem?

_____
_____
_____
_____
_____
_____

Question: What was Festus's response?

_____

_____

_____

_____

_____

_____

Question: What happened after Festus had been in the province for ten days?

_____

_____

_____

_____

_____

_____

Question: What did the Jews do against Paul when he was brought to Festus?

_____

_____

_____

_____

_____

_____

_____

_____

_____

_____

Question: What did Festus do to please the Jews?

_____

_____

_____

_____

_____

_____

Question: How did Paul respond?

_____

_____

_____

_____

_____

_____

_____

_____

_____

_____

_____

Question: To whom did Festus send Paul?

_____

_____

_____

_____

_____

Question: Who came to salute Festus?

_____

_____

_____

_____

_____

_____

Question: What did Festus say to exonerate himself to Agrippa and Bernice?

_____

_____

_____

_____

_____

_____

Question: Whom did Paul want to go before? How did Agrippa respond?

_____

_____

_____

_____

_____

_____

_____

_____

_____

_____

Question: The next day, how did Agrippa and Bernice enter the courtroom?

_____

_____

_____

_____

_____

_____

Question: What did Festus request of Agrippa?

_____

_____

_____

_____

_____

_____

Action: Every day this week, review the six stages to developing patience and read the accompanying scriptures:

1. **Testing:** Patience is developed through testing. "My brethren, count it all joy when ye fall into divers temptations; knowing this, that the trying of your faith worketh patience" (James 1:2–3 KJV).
2. **Waiting:** Patience is developed through waiting. "Rest in the LORD, and wait patiently for him: fret not thyself because of him who prospereth in his way, because of the man who

bringeth wicked devices to pass" (Psalm 37:7 KJV). "And let us not be weary in well doing: for in due season we shall reap, if we faint not" (Galatians 6:9 KJV).

3. **Standing:** Patience is developed by standing on God's promises. "For all the promises of God in him are yea, and in him Amen, unto the glory of God by us" (2 Corinthians 1:20 KJV).

4. **Praying:** Patience is developed through prayer. "And he spake a parable unto them to this end, that men ought always to pray, and not to faint" (Luke 18:1 KJV).

5. **Remembering:** Patience is developed by remembering God's sovereignty. "For my thoughts are not your thoughts, neither are your ways my ways, saith the LORD" (Isaiah 55:8 KJV).

6. **Anticipating**: Patience is developed through anticipating the direction of God. "Trust in the LORD with all thine heart; and lean not unto thine own understanding. In all thy ways acknowledge him, and he shall direct thy paths" (Proverbs 3:5–6 KJV).

Chapter 25 Notes

_____

_____

_____

_____

_____

_____

_____

_____

_____

_____

_____

_____

_____

_____

_____

_____

_____

_____

_____

_____

_____

_____

_____

_____

_____

_____

Creating Consistent Lives
(Chapter 26 Questions)

Question: How did Paul begin his defense to Agrippa?

_____

_____

_____

_____

_____

_____

Question: How did Paul flatter Agrippa?

_____

_____

_____

_____

_____

Question: What does Paul do in Acts 26:4–18?

_____

_____

_____

_____

_____

_____

_____

_____

_____

_____

_____

Question: To whom did Paul say he was obedient?

_____

_____

_____

_____

_____

Question: Who did Paul say helped him to be a witness?

_____

_____

_____

_____

_____

Question: What does Paul say about Christ in Acts 26:23?

_____

_____

_____

_____

_____

_____

Question: How did Festus respond?

_____

_____

_____

_____

_____

_____

_____

_____

_____

_____

_____

Question: How did Paul convict Festus?

_____

_____

_____

_____

_____

_____

_____

_____

_____

_____

_____

_____

Question: What was Festus's response to Paul reminding him about his belief in the prophets?

_____

_____

_____

_____

_____

_____

_____

_____

_____

_____

Question: What was Paul's desire for those who heard him speak?

_____

_____

_____

_____

_____

_____

Question: To what agreement did the council come in a private meeting?

_____

_____

_____

_____

_____

_____

_____

_____

_____

_____

_____

Question: What did Agrippa conclude at the end of the chapter?

_____

_____

_____

_____

_____

_____

_____

_____

_____

_____

_____

Action: Being faithful means being consistent, but remember: the Holy Spirit will help us as we pursue consistency in our spiritual lives. Work toward consistency by examining where your commitments are, exercising good content, and expressing your convictions!

Chapter 26 Notes

_____

_____

_____

_____

_____

_____

_____

_____

_____

_____

_____

_____

_____

_____

_____

_____

_____

_____

_____

_____

_____

_____

_____

_____

_____

_____

Confidence for Life's Dark Storms
(Chapter 27 Questions)

Question: To whom were Paul and the other prisoners delivered?

Question: How did Julius treat Paul?

Question: Why did the ship sail to Cyprus?

_____

_____

_____

_____

_____

_____

Question: What happened when a ship was discovered sailing to Italy?

_____

_____

_____

_____

_____

_____

Question: What was Paul's warning in Fair Havens?

_____

_____

_____

_____

_____

_____

Question: What was the centurion's response to Paul's warning?

_____

_____

_____

_____

_____

_____

Question: What was the name of the wind that arose? How did the sailors try to lighten the ship?

_____

_____

_____

_____

_____

_____

Question: What happened to the sailors after many days without sun or stars?

_____

_____

_____

_____

_____

_____

Question: How did Paul encourage the sailors?

_____

_____

_____

_____

_____

_____

Question: Who did Paul say stood with him?

_____

_____

_____

_____

_____

_____

Question: What was Paul told?

_____

_____

_____

_____

_____

Question: What happened on the fourteenth night?

_____

_____

_____

_____

_____

Question: What were the sailors afraid of hitting?

_____

_____

_____

_____

_____

Question: How many anchors were dropped?

_____

_____

_____

_____

_____

_____

Question: What was Paul's advice to those on the ship?

_____

_____

_____

_____

_____

_____

_____

_____

_____

_____

Question: How does this chapter conclude?

_____

_____

_____

_____

_____

_____

_____

_____

_____

_____

_____

Group Discussion Questions

Question: When seasons of life's dark storms arise in your life, you will need some internal anchors if you are to survive the storm. Paul discovered through the Holy Spirit not to trust external anchors. In what or whom do you put your confidence in during life's dark, raging storms?

_____

_____

_____

_____

_____

_____

_____

_____

_____

_____

Action: When storms or challenges arise, practice leaning on your internal (and eternal) anchors instead of on the external anchors that fail!

Chapter 27 Notes

A Consistent Conclusion
(Chapter 28 Questions)

Question: On what island did Paul and the others land?

_____

_____

_____

_____

_____

_____

Question: What was the attitude of the natives?

_____

_____

_____

_____

_____

_____

Question: What did they do for the sailors?

_____

_____

_____

_____

_____

_____

Question: What happened to Paul as he assisted?

_____

_____

_____

_____

_____

Question: Why were the natives amazed at Paul? What did they call Paul?

_____

_____

_____

_____

_____

Question: What did Paul do for Publius?

_____

_____

_____

_____

_____

_____

Question: What happened when word got around about Paul?

_____

_____

_____

_____

_____

_____

Question: How long did they stay on the island?

_____

_____

_____

_____

_____

_____

Question: What happened when the Egyptian ship came?

_____

_____

_____

_____

_____

_____

Question: What happened when Paul reached Rome?

_____

_____

_____

_____

_____

_____

_____

_____

_____

_____

_____

Question: What happened three days later?

_____

_____

_____

_____

_____

Question: How did the meeting with the Jewish leaders in Rome turn out?

_____

_____

_____

_____

_____

_____

_____
_____
_____
_____
_____
_____

Question: What happened when Paul had the opportunity to share the gospel?

_____
_____
_____
_____
_____
_____
_____
_____
_____
_____
_____

Question: What did Paul say about the Holy Spirit and the prophets?

_____
_____
_____
_____
_____

_____

_____

_____

_____

_____

_____

Question: How does this chapter conclude for Paul?

_____

_____

_____

_____

_____

_____

_____

_____

_____

_____

_____

Group Discussion Questions

Question: How do you handle life when your present predicament does not match your promised future?

_____

_____

_____

_____

_____

_____

_____

_____

_____

_____

_____

_____

Question: How do you remain consistent in inconsistent conditions?

_____

_____

_____

_____

_____

_____

_____

_____

_____

_____

Action: When life throws curve balls at you, lean on the Holy Spirit for consistency and remind yourself that God demands faith, not success, in all circumstances!

Chapter 28 Notes

_____

_____

_____

_____

_____

_____

_____

_____

_____

_____

_____

_____

_____

_____

_____

_____

_____

_____

_____

_____

_____

About the Author

The Reverend Dr. Oscar Terrance Moses is the second child of the late Oscar Moses and Rosetta Moses-Hill and the fifth generation to preach the gospel. He serves as the 17th Pastor of the Mt. Hermon Missionary Baptist Church, where his grandfather, the late Reverend Joseph A. Allen, served as pastor for 41 years.

Dr. Moses is a graduate of Mendel Catholic Preparatory High School of Chicago. He earned his Bachelor of Science Degree in Criminal Justice with a minor in Religious Studies from Southern Illinois University in Carbondale. On June 6, 2000, he received his Master of Arts in Theological Studies from McCormick Theological Seminary. On May 21, 2001, he received a Certificate of Completion for one extended unit of level one CPE by the Association for Clinical Pastoral Education, Inc. at Advocate South Suburban Hospital. Dr. Moses is a Mckissick Carter Fellow graduate of the United Theological Seminary, where he earned his Doctor of Ministry Degree in 2014. His dissertation was focused on *Preaching That Challenges Congregations to Transform Community Hopelessness to Hope and Beyond.*

Dr. Moses married his helpmeet, Jacqueline Marie, on July 27, 1996. She has earned a master's degree in Special Education from Saint Xavier University in Chicago as well as a doctoral degree in Educational Psychology from National Lewis University in Skokie, Illinois.

Dr. Moses has a passion for soul-winning. His commitment to teaching the Word of God has inspired the development of W.A.R. (**W**ord of God **A**pplied **R**ightly) Bible Study.

Dr. Moses is the President and CEO of Exodus Unlimited. The mission of Exodus Unlimited is to glorify our Lord and Savior, Jesus Christ, through community empowerment. On January 17, 2007, the University of Chicago Hospital recognized Exodus Unlimited during the Dr. Martin Luther King Jr. Awards Ceremony for providing After School Care to youth within the Auburn Gresham Community. The After School Care Program was created to reduce educational apathy, gang activity, and low reading scores within the community.

Dr. Moses serves as Moderator for the Christian Unity Baptist District Association. He is the Chairman of Evangelism for the Illinois National Baptist State Convention and the former Coordinator for the Evangelical Board Tent Revival for the National Baptist Convention of America, Inc. Dr. Moses is currently an adjunct professor at Trinity Christian College in Palos, Illinois, teaching "Christian Worldview." Dr. Moses is a member of Omega Psi Phi Inc. Fraternity.

Dr. Moses is a Bible-believing, God-trusting, and God-fearing servant of the Lord. His favorite scripture is: "Trust in the Lord with all thine heart; and lean not unto thine own understanding. In all thy ways acknowledge him, and he shall direct thy paths" (Proverbs 3:5-6 KJV). It is evident that God is truly directing his path as he continues to serve Him in spirit and in truth.

About Sermon To Book

SermonToBook.com began with a simple belief: that sermons should be touching lives, *not* collecting dust. That's why we turn sermons into high-quality books that are accessible to people all over the globe.

Turning your sermon series into a book exposes more people to God's Word, better equips you for counseling, accelerates future sermon prep, adds credibility to your ministry, and even helps make ends meet during tight times.

John 21:25 tells us that the world itself couldn't contain the books that would be written about the work of Jesus Christ. Our mission is to try anyway. Because, in heaven, there will no longer be a need for sermons or books. Our time is now.

If God so leads you, we'd love to work with you on your sermon or sermon series.

Visit www.sermontobook.com to learn more.